Calculator Activities
MEASUREMENT

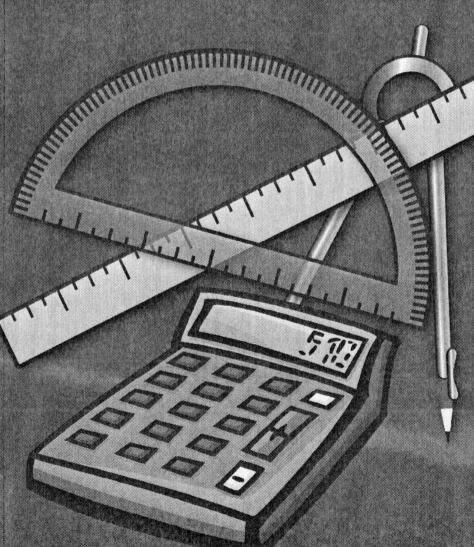

- Give students real-world understanding of measurement
- Provide different techniques and tools for solving problems
- Teach units, processes, and systems of measurement
- Allow students to explore calculator functions

Carrie S. Cutler, Ed.D.
Illustrated by David Parker

Copyright ©2007 Prufrock Press Inc.

Edited by Lacy Elwood
Editorial Assistant: Kate Sepanski
Production Design by Marjorie Parker
Illustrated by David Parker

ISBN-13: 978-1-59363-223-6
ISBN-10: 1-59363-223-1

Prufrock Press Inc.
P.O. Box 8813
Waco, TX 76714-8813
Phone: (800) 998-2208
Fax: (800) 240-0333
http://www.prufrock.com

Contents

Teacher's Guide: Introduction

I hope the lessons in this book will open your students' eyes to the real world of measurement. Measurement is more than inches on a ruler. We use measurement to keep track of cafeteria accounts, paper in the classroom cupboard, and time remaining on a favorite video game. Using the calculator helps us move beyond computation to solve real-world measurement problems like: *How much pizza can we afford? Will we have time to ride all of our favorite roller coasters?* and *How much colder is it in Antarctica than in our classroom?*

By third grade, most students have experience with measurable attributes such as time, money (value), temperature, length, volume, area, and weight (mass). They also have experience comparing objects to one another and to a unit of measure, often a nonstandard unit. Building upon prior learning, the majority of the measurement tasks in this book focus on the National Council of Teachers of Mathematics (NCTM) expectations for measurement. According to the NTCM, students should see the need for standardized units of measurement, use benchmarks to make reasonable estimates, and develop and understand simple formulas for measurement. Teachers should provide rich mathematical tasks from which students may develop problem solving and reasoning. The tasks in this book will enable your students to make investigations and build mathematical knowledge by solving problems that arise in real-world contexts.

This book may be used as a supplement to the regular curriculum or as an extension for gifted students in grades 3–6. Each lesson includes a Teacher's Guide, as well as worksheets for students. Each lesson's Teacher's Guide offers suggestions for vocabulary development, facilitation questions to guide student discovery of mathematical concepts, and an answer key.

The student worksheets can be completed individually or by small groups of students.

Whether used as elaboration on a previously learned topic or as an introduction to a new mathematical concept, this book provides an avenue for implementing technology into the mathematics classroom and makes the real world of mathematics accessible to your students. Many teachers are unsure of when to allow students to use calculators. Through these tasks, students are prompted to use the calculator as a tool for problem solving. Of course, computation that can be completed quickly and accurately using mental strategies should still be reinforced. However, the tasks in this book have been developed to help students see the usefulness of the calculator to look for patterns, deal with very large or very small numbers, solve complex computations, and so forth. By using the calculator as a problem-solving strategy, this book gives students access to real-world contexts and numbers and extends the range of problems they can successfully solve.

You can assess your students' work using the Generalized Scoring Rubric in Appendix A of this book. You can use this rubric to evaluate the "big picture" of student understanding and communication of mathematical ideas. In addition, you may use the answer key included at the end of each lesson to help score students' work. Another item that may be helpful during the course of teaching this book's activities is the Links to Literature Guide in Appendix B.

I hope you find this book helpful in incorporating calculators into your classroom. I hope the real-world contexts allow students to see the everyday applications for measurement. Most of all, I hope the students find the lessons too fun to measure. Enjoy!

Atop the Drop Kick Coaster
Teacher's Guide

Measurement Concept: Time

Calculator Focus: Examining data and relationships

Materials:
- Atop the Drop Kick Coaster worksheet (one per group; pp. 7–9)
- calculators
- grid paper
- crayons or markers
- chart paper
- ruler

Procedure: Students will work in partners to complete the questions on the Atop the Drop Kick Coaster worksheet. Teachers can use the facilitation questions below to help guide the students as they complete the worksheet.

Vocabulary:
- *circle graph:* a graph in the shape of a circle, or pie, that shows how a total amount has been divided into parts. The circle represents the total amount. The slices of "pie" show how the total amount has been divided.

Facilitation Questions:
- *What do you need to know to figure out how long you must wait for your turn on the Drop Kick?*
- *What considerations will go into making your plan for how you'll spend your time at the park?*
- *What are the benefits of your first plan? What are the drawbacks?*
- *How does your second plan compare to your first plan? Is one plan better than the other? How?*
- *How does a circle graph help us see how the wait time compares to the riding time?*
- *What do you need to know to construct your circle graph?*
- *What does the whole circle represent?*
- *What labels do you need to include on your circle graph?*
- *What mathematical and problem-solving processes did you use during the activity?*

Answer Key:
1. 7 hours
2. 14 minutes
3. The Rocky Top Railroad. Explanations will vary.
4. Answers will vary. Students must include each coaster at least once. Students should develop two plans. Explanations should show reasoning and problem solving, as well as correct computation. This step may be scored using the Generalized Scoring Rubric in Appendix A.
5. Answers will vary.
6. This means we spent the least time on this ride.
7. The longest strip will invariably be the white strip. This means that most of our time is spent waiting in line rather than riding on roller coasters.
8. Answers will vary. The circle graph should be similar to the graph created with the grid strips and labeled correctly.
9. Written explanations will vary but should express the reasoning and problem solving that the student used during the activity. The writing portion can be graded using the Generalized Scoring Rubric or a rubric created in cooperation with the students prior to the activity.

Name:_____ Date:_____

Atop the Drop Kick Coaster

You and a friend won free passes to the amusement park. Forget the kiddie rides—you and your pal want some thrills! The park has five different roller coasters. Using your calculator and the information from the table, answer the questions below.

> **The Problem:** How could we figure out the best combinations of rides for our day at the amusement park?

1. Your friend's mom drops you off at the front gate of the amusement park at 11 a.m. The park closes at 6 p.m. How much time will you spend at the park?

The table below shows the rides, the number of people in line, how many people each ride can carry, and the length of the ride, including time for loading and unloading. Use this information to determine the answers to the next few questions.

Name of Roller Coaster	Number of People in Line in Front of You	Ride Capacity	Length of Ride (Including Loading/ Unloading)
Roller Express	88	12	5 minutes
Spin City	99	24	3 minutes
Hang Time	27	6	4 minutes
Drop Kick	34	16	7 minutes
Rocky Top Railroad	71	14	5 minutes

2. How long will you have to wait for your turn on the Drop Kick?

3. Which ride would you be able to get on sooner, the Roller Express or the Rocky Top Railroad? Explain your thinking.

4. Look back at **The Problem** listed in the box on the first page of the lesson. Work with your partner to create two different plans for how you could spend your time at the amusement park. Be sure to include: (a) each ride at least once, (b) the total number of minutes in line and the total number of minutes riding on roller coasters, and (c) the benefits and drawbacks of each combination. Write your plans and explanations on a separate piece of paper.

5. Choose one of your plans for how you could spend your time at the amusement park. Follow the directions below to show how much time you would spend waiting and how much time you would spend on each ride.
   a. Count the number of minutes you spend riding the Roller Express. Use grid paper to make a strip representing the number of minutes.
   b. Color the grids for riding the Roller Express red.
   c. Repeat steps a and b for each roller coaster ride. Choose a different color for each ride's strip of grid paper.
   d. Make a strip of grid paper to represent the total number of minutes you spend waiting. Leave the grid for waiting white.

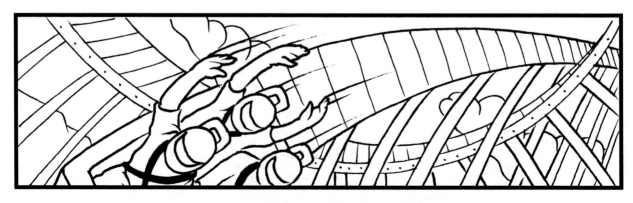

Name:_____ Date:_____

6. Compare the strips. Which color strip is the shortest? Why?

7. Which strip is the longest? What does this mean?

8. Tape all of the colored and white strips into one long strip, then tape the ends together to form a circle. Place the circle on its edge on a sheet of chart paper. Use a crayon or marker to trace around the outside edge of the circle. Create a circle graph by drawing lines to show the separate color sections. Label the sections or color in the sections accordingly.

9. What are three important ideas you learned from figuring out the best combinations of rides for your day at the amusement park?

Between a Rock and a Hard Place
Teacher's Guide

Measurement Concepts: Length, perimeter, area, conversion within a system

Calculator Focus: Exploring place value

Materials:
- Beneath a Rock and a Hard Place worksheet (one per group; pp. 12–16)
- calculators
- newspaper
- rulers
- string
- centimeter grid paper
- centimeter cubes
- access to landscape rocks or the Bugs Under a Rock reproducible (p. 17)

Procedure: Students will work in partners or small groups of three to complete the Beneath a Rock and a Hard Place worksheet. Teachers can use the facilitation questions below to help guide the students as they complete the worksheet. Teachers should take students to a rocky flowerbed or other area in the school to measure the rocks, set up a false flowerbed with rocks and fake bugs for students to use, or give students the Bugs Under a Rock reproducible.

Vocabulary:
- *perimeter*: the distance around a shape or figure.
- *length*: usually refers to the measurement of the distance from one end of any object or space to the other.
- *width*: the measurement of an object from side to side.
- *area*: the measurement of the space enclosed by a figure, expressed in square units.
- *square unit*: a square with each side equal to one unit.
- *centimeter*: a unit of length in the metric system of measurement.

- *meter*: a unit of length in the metric system of measurement; one meter equals 100 centimeters.

Facilitation Questions:
- *What benchmarks do you have for one centimeter?*
- *Which tool would be appropriate for measuring length and width?*
- *Which side of the ruler shows centimeters?*
- *Why is it difficult to use the ruler to measure perimeter?*
- *How does your tracing compare to the actual dimensions of your rock?*
- *What patterns do you see on your table?*
- *Have we accounted for each of the rocks around the flowerbed?*
- *What ideas did you use to help make your estimate of the total number of bugs? How do you know that your estimate is reasonable? What information from the table is most helpful in making an estimate?*

Answer Key:
1. Answers will vary.
2. Length + width = half the perimeter. Or, length + length + width + width = perimeter.
4. Answers will vary.
5. If the rock is a rectangular shape, the area could be calculated by multiplying length times width. If the rock is more triangular, the area could be calculated by multiplying one half of the base times height.
6. Answers will vary.
7. The area of the rock could be sectioned off into square centimeters or covered with centimeter cubes.
8. One measure may be more accurate than another, but no measurement is precise. There is always another, smaller unit that will give a more precise measurement.
9. Answers will vary.
10. Answers will vary.
11. To estimate the total perimeter of the rocks, students could figure an average perimeter of all the rocks measured and

multiply that by the total number of rocks in the flowerbed.

12. To estimate the total area, students could find an average measurement of the rocks' area.

13. Answers will vary.

14. There are 100 centimeters in one meter. Using a calculator, students could divide by 100 to find the number of meters in each of the centimeter measurements.

15. Answers will vary.

16. To estimate the total number of insects living under the rocks, students could figure an average number of insects they counted and multiply that number by the total number of rocks in the flowerbed.

Name:_____ Date:_____

Between a Rock and a Hard Place

Decorative rocks surround the flowerbeds in front of our school. The rocks provide a habitat for many insects. We want to figure out approximately how many insects call those rocks "home sweet home."

> **The Problem:** How could we figure out how many insects live under the rocks surrounding our school's flowerbed?

Use the chart below as you complete this lesson.

	Length of Rock	Width of Rock	Perimeter of Rock	Area of Rock	Number of Insects
Estimate					
Actual					

1. Choose a rock. Estimate the length and width of the rock in centimeters. Select the appropriate tool and measure the length and width of your rock in centimeters. Record your estimates and the actual length and width on the chart above.

2. Estimate the perimeter of your rock. Use a piece of string and a ruler to measure the perimeter of your rock in centimeters. Record your estimate and the actual perimeter on the table. What relationship do you see between the length, width, and perimeter?

3. Place a piece of newspaper over your rock. Trace a rough outline. Cut out the tracing.

Name:_____ Date:_____

4. Brainstorm with your partner possible strategies for calculating the area of your rock. Record your ideas here.

5. How could you use your calculator and the information from the table to figure the area of your rock? Describe one method and calculate your area this way.

6. Think of another approach that also would work. Describe it, then calculate your area this way.

7. How could you use your tracing to figure the area of your rock?

8. Cover your tracing with centimeter cubes or transfer your tracing to centimeter grid paper. Count the cubes required to cover the rock. How does this figure compare with the area you calculated in Question 5? Why might it differ?

9. Estimate the number of insects you think live under your rock. Carefully lift your rock and count the insects you see. Be cautious to return the rock to its original position afterward. Record your estimate and the actual number of insects on the chart provided at the beginning of the lesson.

Name:_____ Date:_____

10. Work as a class to compile all of the groups' measurements into a new table. Fill in the table below.

Whole Class Table

Length of Rock	Width of Rock	Perimeter of Rock	Area of Rock	Number of Insects
Group 1				
Group 2				
Group 3				
Group 4				
Group 5				
Group 6				
Group 7				
Group 8				
Estimated Total (cm)				
Actual Total (cm)				
Estimated Total (meters)				
Actual Total (meters)				

11. Use the Whole Class Table you created in Question 10 to estimate the total perimeter of all the rocks in centimeters. Use your calculator to figure the actual total perimeter in centimeters.

Estimate: _____ Actual: _____

12. Estimate the total area in centimeters. Use your calculator to figure the actual total area in centimeters.

Estimate: _____ Actual: _____

13. Estimate the total number of insects living under the rocks in our flowerbed.

14. What is the relationship between centimeters and meters? How could your calculator help you determine the actual perimeter and area in meters?

15. Look back at **The Problem** listed in the box on the first page of the lesson. If the class has counted all of the insects under all of the rocks around the flowerbed, record the total number of insects living under the rocks surrounding our school's flowerbeds.

16. If there are still rocks that haven't been lifted and the insects beneath them haven't been counted, how could you use the information from the Whole Class Table to estimate the total number of insects that live under the rocks surrounding our school's flowerbeds? Write a sentence about your strategy and record your estimate below.

My Strategy:

My Estimate: _____

Name:_____ Date:_____

Bugs Under A Rock

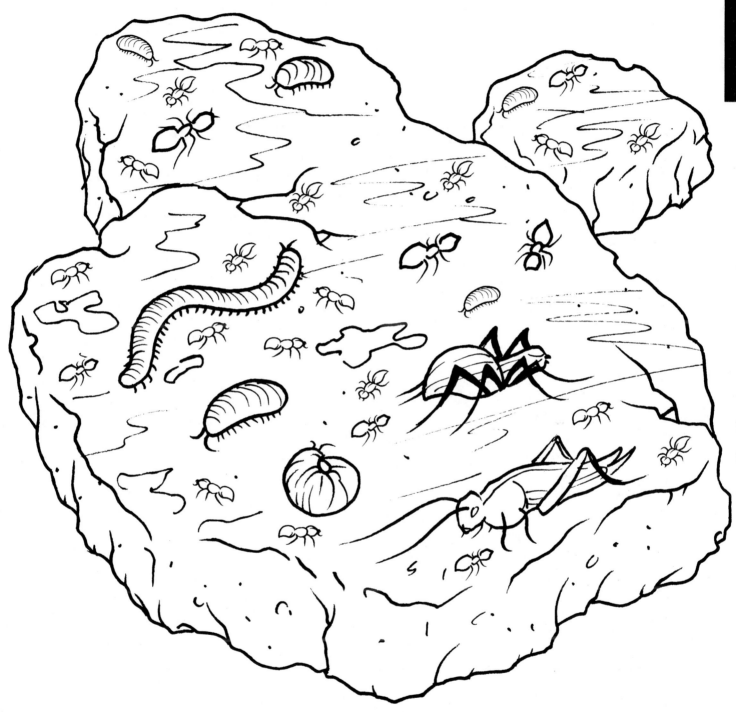

Down the Highway
Teacher's Guide

Measurement Concepts: Length, benchmarks for distance, liquid capacity, money

Calculator Focus: Examining number magnitude

Materials:
- Down the Highway worksheets (one per group; pp. 20–24)
- calculators
- rulers
- road maps or atlases of the United States
- small map of the U.S. (p. 25)
- access to information about fuel prices

Procedure: Students will work in partners or small groups of three to complete the Down the Highway worksheet. Teachers can use the facilitation questions below to help guide the students as they complete the worksheet.

Vocabulary:
- *mile*: a unit of length in the customary system of measurement; one mile equals 5,280 feet or 1,760 yards.
- *gallon*: a unit of capacity in the customary system of measurement; one gallon equals 4 quarts.
- *miles per gallon*: a measure of the fuel efficiency of a vehicle; the number of miles a vehicle can drive on one gallon of fuel.

Facilitation Questions:
- *What resources could you use to find out the location of South Dakota on the map?*
- *Which states border South Dakota?*
- *How could you find out the location of Rapid City or Mount Rushmore on the map?*
- *Do you have any benchmarks that may help you in estimating the distance from Houston to Mount Rushmore?*
- *How could plotting your route on a road map of the United States help you find the shortest route? How could using your calculator help you find the shortest route?*

- *How many major cities are on your route?*
- *How did using a benchmark for long distances improve your estimate for the distance from Houston to Mount Rushmore?*
- *How does the information in the table and the total number of miles on your planned route help you figure out how many gallons of gas each type of vehicle will need for the trip?*
- *Is one type of fuel cheaper than the other? How does this affect the total cost of the trip?*

Answer Key:

1–3. See the map indicating South Dakota, Mount Rushmore, and Houston.

4. Using a benchmark for distance helps make a reasonable estimate.

6. The shortest route using this chart is:
> City 1: Dallas, TX
> City 2: Oklahoma City, OK
> City 3: Wichita, KS
> City 4: Topeka, KS
> City 5: Kansas City, MO
> City 6: Sioux Falls, SD
> City 7: Rapid City, SD

The total number of miles for the route given is 1,523 miles.

7–9. Answers will vary.

10.

Vehicle	Number of Vehicles Needed	Miles per Gallon	Total Gallons Needed
School Bus (60 passengers)	1	8 miles per gallon	380.75 gallons
Rented Tour Bus (50 passengers)	1	6 miles per gallon	507.67 gallons
Van (12 passengers)	4	18 miles per gallon	676.89 gallons
Car (5 passengers)	8	25 miles per gallon	974.72 gallons

11–13. Answers will vary.

14.

Vehicle	Total Gallons Needed for Round-Trip	Cost of Fuel per Gallon	Total Cost of Fuel for Trip	Other Expenses	Total Cost
School Bus	380.75 gallons	will vary	will vary	None	will vary
Rented Tour Bus	507.67 gallons	will vary	will vary	$500 rental fee	will vary
12-Passenger Vans	676.89 gallons	will vary	will vary	$280 rental fee	will vary
Cars	974.72 gallons	will vary	will vary	None	will vary

15. Answers will vary.

16. Answers will vary. Score the letter to the fifth graders at Johnson Elementary using the Generalized Scoring Rubric.

Down the Highway

The fifth-grade class at Johnson Elementary School in Houston, TX, is planning a field trip to Mount Rushmore in South Dakota. We want to help them figure out (a) approximately how far it is from Houston to Mount Rushmore, (b) how much gasoline it will take to get there, and (c) which type of vehicle will be most efficient on the trip.

> **The Problem:** How could we figure out the shortest route and best transportation for the students' field trip?

1. Mount Rushmore is located in South Dakota. Find South Dakota on the map of the United States and outline it.

2. The closest major city to Mount Rushmore is Rapid City. Draw a dot on the state of South Dakota to show where Mount Rushmore is located.

3. Johnson Elementary is located in Houston, TX. Find Houston on the map and draw a dot to show where it is located. How many miles do you think it is from Houston to Mount Rushmore? Write your estimate here.

4. Do you have any benchmarks for long distances? Maybe you have a general idea of the number of miles you travel when you go to visit family or friends that live far away. How could using your benchmarks for distance help you estimate the number of miles from Houston to Mount Rushmore?

Name:_____ Date:_____

5. The fifth-grade class will be driving to Mount Rushmore, so they need help planning the shortest route. Use the table below and a calculator to plan a route you think the class should take to get to Mount Rushmore in Rapid City, SD.

Major Cities on the Route	Approximate Distance	Freeway Name
Dallas, TX	247 miles from Houston	Interstate 45
Oklahoma City, OK	208 miles from Dallas	Interstate 35
Wichita, KS	157 miles from Oklahoma City	Interstate 35
Denver, CO	521 miles from Wichita	Interstate 70
Topeka, KS	136 miles from Wichita	Interstate 35
Kansas City, MO	54 from Topeka	Interstate 70
Cheyenne, WY	100 miles from Denver	Interstate 25
Sioux Falls, SD	373 miles from Kansas City	Interstate 29
Casper, WY	180 from Cheyenne	Interstate 25
Rapid City, SD	242 miles from Casper 348 miles from Sioux Falls	Interstates 25 & 90 Interstate 90

6. Write your route here. (You may not need all nine slots.)

City 1:

City 2:

City 3:

City 4:

City 5:

City 6:

City 7:

City 8:

City 9:

Rapid City, SD, at last!

Total number of miles: _____

7. How does your estimate from Question 3 compare to the actual number of miles from Houston to Mount Rushmore? Use an atlas or distance calculator on the Internet to find out exactly how many miles it is from Houston to Mount Rushmore.

8. What type of reasoning went into planning your route?

9. Why did you choose this route instead of the other options?

10. The fifth graders have four options for driving to Mount Rushmore. They can take a school bus, a rented tour bus, vans, or cars driven by parents. Use a calculator to complete the table below. Keep in mind that there are 30 fifth graders and 10 adults going on the field trip and that you have to calculate the amount of gas needed for both the trip there and the trip back.

Vehicle	Number of Vehicles Needed	Miles per Gallon	Total Gallons Needed
School Bus (maximum 60 passengers)		8 miles per gallon	
Rented Tour Bus (maximum 50 passengers)		6 miles per gallon	
Van (maximum 12 passengers)		18 miles per gallon	
Car (maximum 5 passengers)		25 miles per gallon	

11. What type of vehicle do you think the class should use to drive to Mount Rushmore?

12. The buses use diesel fuel. The cars and vans use unleaded gasoline. Research the prices of gasoline and diesel and compare the costs.

Price of diesel per gallon: _____

Price of unleaded gasoline per gallon: _____

13. How does the difference in fuel prices affect your travel plans?

14. Use the table below to organize your information about fuel and costs.

Vehicle	Total Gallons Needed for Round-Trip	Cost of Fuel per Gallon	Total Cost of Fuel for Trip	Other Expenses	Total Cost
School Bus				None	
Rented Tour Bus				$500 rental fee	
12-Passenger Vans				$280 rental fee	
Cars				None	

Name:_____ Date:_____

15. Based on the information in your table, which type of vehicle do you think would be best for the field trip? Why?

16. On a separate sheet of paper, write a letter to the fifth graders at Johnson Elementary describing how you determined the best route and type of vehicle for the field trip. Include details about how you made your decisions.

© Prufrock Press Inc. • *Calculator Activities: Measurement*
This page may be photocopied or reproduced with permission for student use.

Name: _____ Date: _____

In the Garden Patch
Teacher's Guide

Measurement Concept: Area formulas for quadrilaterals

Calculator Focus: Detecting patterns in formulas

Materials:
- In the Garden Patch worksheet (one per group; pp. 27–30)
- calculators
- several sheets of ½-inch grid paper
- tape or glue
- large sheets of construction paper

Procedure: Students will work in partners or small groups of three to complete the In the Garden worksheet. Teachers can use the facilitation questions below to help guide the students as they complete the worksheet.

Vocabulary:
- *square unit:* a square with each side equal to one unit.
- *foot:* a unit of length in the customary system of measurement; one foot equals 12 inches.
- *square foot:* equal to the area of a square that measures one foot on each side.
- *area:* the measurement of the space enclosed by a figure, expressed in square units.
- *height:* the measurement of an object vertically from one end of the object to the other.
- *base:* the measurement of an object horizontally from end to end.
- *quadrilateral:* a polygon with four sides.

Facilitation Questions:
- *What does the term* area *mean?*
- *How can you figure the area of these figures?*
- *What does the term* height *mean?*
- *What does the term* base *mean?*
- *What arithmetic operation do you find in the relationship between the base and height of a quadrilateral and its area?*
- *The formula for the area of a quadrilateral is length of the base times height. How could you write the formula using symbols rather than words?*
- *Most vegetable gardens are rectangles. Why do you think that is?*
- *How does the shape affect how we plant and take care of our garden?*
- *How many sheets of grid paper will you need to make your garden layout?*
- *What strategies can you use to organize your calculations?*

Answer Key:

1.

Type of Quadrilateral	Area (Square Units)	Base (Units)	Height (Units)
A. Square	4	2	2
B. Rectangle	10	5	2
C. Rectangle	6	3	2
D. Square	9	3	3
E. Rectangle	6	6	1

2. The base multiplied by the height equals the number of square units (the area) for the quadrilateral.

3. Area equals base multiplied by height.
   a. 3,108 square feet
   b. 57,600 square feet
   c. 12,350 square feet

4. Some possible dimensions include: 30 x 10, 15 x 20, 50 x 6, 60 x 5, 300 x 1, 100 x 3. Students may also reverse the order of the dimensions.

5. Answers may include ideas about ease of planting, weeding, and watering or playground space considerations.

6. Students' layouts may resemble the Square Foot Method shown in the illustration below.

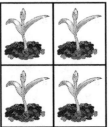

7. Answers will vary.

26

Name:_____ Date:_____

In the Garden Patch

Our principal will allow us to use 300 square feet of playground space for our class garden plot. We want to plant at least five different vegetables. Work as a group to design the best shape for our plot and to select which vegetables to plant.

The Problem: How could we figure out the best shape, size, and vegetables for our garden plot?

1. Look at the quadrilaterals below. Fill in the table that follows.

A.

B.

C.

D.

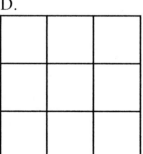

E.

Type of Quadrilateral	Area (Square Units)	Base (Units)	Height (Units)
A.			
B.			
C.			
D.			
E.			

2. What is the pattern you find between the base and height of a quadrilateral and the quadrilateral's area?

3. Based on the patterns you found in Question 2, make a formula to find the area of a quadrilateral. Then use your calculator to find the area of the sports fields below:

My area formula:

a. The area of a basketball court:
   Base = 74 feet   Height = 42 feet   Area =

b. The area of a football field:
   Base = 360 feet   Height = 160 feet   Area =

c. The area of a soccer field:
   Base = 130 feet   Height = 95 feet   Area =

Name:_____ Date:_____

4. Our principal will let us use a section of the playground with an area of 300 square feet. Use a calculator to find some possible shapes and dimensions for our garden plot. Fill in the table below to show your ideas.

Shape	Base	Height	Area
			300
			300
			300
			300
			300
			300
			300

5. Some of the quadrilaterals from the table on Question 4 are long and skinny. Some of the quadrilaterals are short and wide. Discuss with your group which quadrilateral you think will be the best for our garden. Then, write a paragraph about your group's decision on a separate sheet of paper.

Name:_____ Date:_____

6. Look back at **The Problem** listed on the first page of the lesson. Draw a map of your garden on grid paper using the shape your group decided on in Question 5. Each unit on the grid paper equals one square foot. Leave a space of one foot between rows so that we have room to walk between them to plant, weed, and water. Then, use the table below to help you choose which vegetables to plant in our garden and where to plant them. Remember we want to plant at least five different types of vegetables.

7. We won't have to wait for our plants to grow from tiny seeds. A local nursery will give our class a special price on vegetable starter plants that have been grown in cups in the greenhouse. Use the price information in the table below and your calculator to figure out how much it will cost to plant your garden.

Total cost of planting our garden: $_____

Type of Plant	Distance Between Plants	Does Well Near	Does Not Do Well Near	Cost per Plant
Beans	6 inches	carrots, potatoes	onions	$1.07
Cabbage	18 inches	carrots, onions, potatoes	beans, tomatoes	$1.27
Potatoes	12 inches	beans, carrots	tomatoes	$0.97
Onions	4 inches	cabbage, tomatoes	beans	$0.79
Peas	4 inches	potatoes, beans, corn	onions	$0.55
Corn	18 inches (For pollination, corn must be planted in at least four rows.)	beans, cabbage	does well near anything	$0.89
Tomatoes	24 inches	carrots, onions	cabbage, potatoes, broccoli	$1.33
Broccoli	12 inches	carrots, onions, potatoes	beans, tomatoes	$1.35

Out to Lunch
Teacher's Guide

Measurement Concepts: Circumference/diameter relationships

Calculator Focus: Detecting patterns in formulas

Materials:

- Out to Lunch worksheet (one per group; pp. 32–35)
- calculators
- measuring tape (or yarn and rulers)

Procedure: Students will work in partners or small groups of three to complete the Out to Lunch worksheet. Teachers can use the facilitation questions below to help guide the students as they complete the worksheet.

Vocabulary:

- *dimension:* measurement or size of a shape or figure.
- *circumference:* the distance around a circle; a little more than three times its diameter.
- *diameter:* the diameter of a circle has a line that passes through the center of the circle and has endpoints on the circle.
- *pi:* the actual ratio of the circumference of a circle to its diameter, with an approximate value of 3.14. To find the circumference (C) of a circle, multiply the diameter (d) of the circle by 3.14 (an approximation of pi). The formula for finding the circumference of a circle may be written as $C = \pi \times d$.
- *formula:* equation expressing a mathematical relationship, principle, or rule.

Facilitation Questions:

- *What other experience have you had figuring diameter and circumference?*
- *How does looking at the table in Question 1 help you know how to find the circumference of a circle?*
- *How can we measure the circumference of a circular face without using measuring tape?*
- *What patterns do you see on your table in Question 1, the circumference of the*

enormous pizza in Question 3, and the results of your measurements in Question 4?

- *By looking at the menu, how much does the restaurant charge per slice of pizza? Does this price change as the pizzas get larger?*
- *What factors would affect how much pizza a person could eat?*
- *How many classmates do you think you should interview? How could you get a representative sample of your classmates?*
- *How could we figure the total cost of the pizzas?*
- *What kind of reasoning went into your decision about which pizzas to buy?*

Answer Key:

1.

	Diameter (d)	Circumference (C)	C + d	C – d	C x d	C/d
Small	9 inches	28.31 inches	37.31 in.	19.31 in.	254.79 in.	3.14 in.
Medium	12 inches	37.72 inches	49.72 in.	25.72 in.	452.64 in.	3.14 in.
Large	15 inches	47.14 inches	62.14 in.	32.14 in.	707.10 in.	3.14 in.
Extra Large	18 inches	56.52 inches	74.52 in.	38.52 in.	1,017.36 in.	3.14 in.

2. Answers will vary. Students should note that the final column (C/D) is 3.14 for all of the pizzas.

3. 65.94 inches.

4. Answers will vary. The circumference should be 3.14 times larger than the diameter of the circles.

5. The circumference of a circle is always exactly 3.14 times larger than its diameter.

7. The Enormous pizza gives you the most slices of pizza for your money. Answers will vary as to reasoning.

8–9. Answers will vary.

10. The student should add the number of slices of pizza, then divide that by the number of classmates interviewed to find the average number of slices of pizza.

11–13. Answers will vary.

Out to Lunch

Our class has been recycling aluminum cans. With the money we have earned, we are going to have a pizza party at Taste of Italy Pizzeria. We need to figure out (a) which size of pizza is the best bargain, (b) how many pizzas we will need, and (c) how much the party will cost.

> **The Problem:** How could we figure out which size of pizza is the best bargain?

1. The table below shows the dimensions for the pizzas we could buy at Taste of Italy Pizzeria. The diameter is the distance across the center of the pizza from edge to edge. The circumference is the distance all the way around the edge of the pizza. Use your calculator to help you fill in the missing boxes on the table.

	Diameter (d)	Circumference (C)	C + d	C − d	C x d	C/d
Small	9 inches	28.31 inches				
Medium	12 inches	37.72 inches				
Large	15 inches	47.14 inches				
Extra Large	18 inches	56.52 inches				

2. What patterns do you notice in the table? Write about your observations.

3. Taste of Italy has just added another size to their menu—Enormous. It has a diameter of 21 inches. Based on what you see in the C/d column, what would the circumference of the Enormous size pizza be?

4. Find three items in the classroom that have a circular face (e.g., clock, paper plate, button, doorknob). Use a measuring tape (or yarn and a ruler) to measure and record the circumference of each item. Use your calculator and, without measuring the object again, figure out and record the diameter of each item.

Item Name	Circumference	Diameter

5. What do you notice about the relationship between the circumference and diameter of a circle?

6. Look at the Taste of Italy Pizzeria menu below. The menu lists the price and number of slices for each pizza.

TASTE OF ITALY PIZZERIA MENU		
Small	6 slices	$5.99
Medium	8 slices	$7.99
Large	10 slices	$9.99
Extra Large	14 slices	$13.99
Enormous	18 slices	$15.99

7. Based on the information in the menu, which size gives you the most slices of pizza for your money? How do you know this?

8. How do we figure out how many pizzas we'll need to buy? Give at least three ideas for how we could figure out how many pizzas we need for our party.

9. Take a survey of the class to find out how many slices of pizza each person will eat. Ask a sample of at least five people. Record the results of the survey in the table.

Name	Number of Slices

10. Use the information in the table and your calculator to find the average number of slices of pizza each person in the sample will eat.

We should plan to buy _____ slices of pizza per person.

11. What other information do we need to consider before we finalize our pizza order?

12. Now that we've figured out how many slices the average person in our class will eat, we need a grand total number of slices needed for the party. Use your calculator to figure out how many slices will we need. Don't forget to include any teachers or staff who will attend the party and any other information that may affect the amount of pizza we need.

We will need to order _____ slices of pizza for our party.

13. Remember that Taste of Italy Pizzeria offers five sizes of pizzas. Also, recall which size of pizza you found to be the best bargain. Then, decide which combination of pizzas will give us enough slices for our party, without having too much left over. For instance, we don't want to spend $15.99 for an Enormous pizza if we only need a few slices. Write about (a) how many of each size of pizza you would order for the party, (b) the total cost of the pizzas, and (c) how you decided which pizzas to buy.

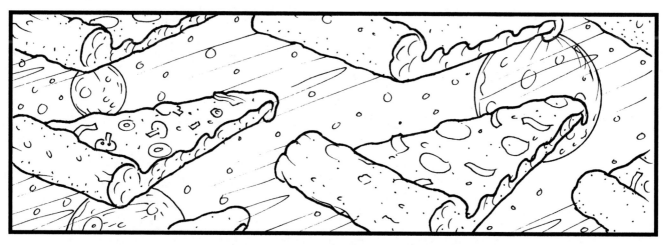

Below Freezing
Teacher's Guide

Measurement Concepts: Temperature

Calculator Focus: Exploring negative numbers, discovering phases of skip counting and number patterns

Materials:
- Below Freezing worksheet (one per group; pp. 37–39)
- calculators
- thermometers (to use as a visual aid)

Procedure: Students will work in partners or small groups of three to complete the Below Freezing worksheet. Teachers can use the facilitation questions below to help guide the students as they complete the worksheet.

Vocabulary:
- *temperature*: a measure of heat or cold. Temperature is measured in degrees Celsius (°C) in the metric system of measurement and degrees Fahrenheit (°F) in the customary system of measurement. The Fahrenheit scale was the primary temperature standard in most English-speaking countries until the late 1960s. The Celsius scale was phased-in as part of the adoption of the metric system.
- *degrees*: a unit of measure for temperature.
- *thermometer*: a tool used to measure temperature.
- *freezing point*: water freezes at 32 degrees Fahrenheit (0 degrees Celsius).
- *negative number*: any number less than 0. Negative numbers are written with a negative sign (-).

Facilitation Questions:
- *Do you have a benchmark for the temperature in the classroom?*
- *Have you read or learned about the climate of Antarctica? Do you think it is slightly colder or much colder than the climate in our area?*
- *Where do numbers that fall below zero appear on a number line?*
- *If you have a thermometer, this may be an appropriate time to show it to the students. What temperature range does the thermometer show?*
- *What can you tell your friend about the temperature in Antarctica?*
- *What type of clothing should your friend pack?*
- *How could you use temperature to help describe negative numbers to your friend?*

Answer Key:
1. Answers will vary. A reasonable response would be between 70 degrees F (21 degrees C) and 80 degrees F (27 degrees C).
2. Answers will vary. A reasonable response would be less than the freezing point, 32 degrees Fahrenheit (0 degrees Celsius).
3. Negative numbers.
4. –50 degrees Fahrenheit.
6. 67 days.
7. Answers will vary. A reasonable response should be fewer than 67 days.
8. At day 4, the temperature will drop below the freezing point to 20 degrees Fahrenheit.
9. At day 6, the temperature will drop below 0 degrees Fahrenheit.
10. 16 days.
11. Answers will vary. Score the letter using the Generalized Scoring Rubric.

Name:_____ Date:_____

Below Freezing

Sometimes in the winter we have to wear jackets or coats. But, in Antarctica, it is cold all of the time. Antarctica is the coldest, highest, windiest, driest, and iciest continent on earth. How many degrees colder is it in Antarctica than in our classroom?

The Problem: How could we figure out what how much colder it is in Antarctica than in our classroom?

---

1. What do you think the temperature is in our classroom? You may use degrees Fahrenheit or degrees Celsius for your estimate. Write your estimate here.

2. How cold do you think it is in Antarctica today? You may use degrees Fahrenheit or degrees Celsius for your estimate. Write your estimate here.

3. Often the temperature in Antarctica falls below 0 degrees Fahrenheit. What are numbers below 0 called?

4. If we laid a thermometer on its side, it would look like a number line. The number line below shows the annual average temperature in degrees Fahrenheit for the interior regions of Antarctica. Write the temperature shown by the dot on the thermometer below.

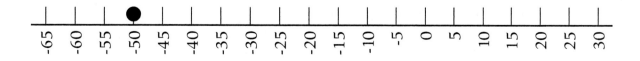

Name:_____ Date:_____

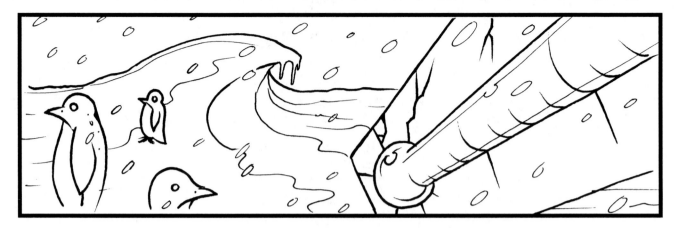

5. The world's coldest temperature was recorded on July 21, 1983, in Vostok, Antarctica. The temperature was −129 degrees Fahrenheit (−89.44 degrees Celsius). That's cold! Imagine that the temperature in our classroom is 72 degrees Fahrenheit and the temperature drops 3 degrees each day. Use the counting constant function feature on your calculator to repeatedly subtract 3 degrees until you reach a temperature of −129 degrees Fahrenheit. Punch the following sequence into your calculator and watch the pattern.

72	−	3	=	=	=

6. How many days will it take to reach the coldest temperature ever recorded if the temperature drops 3 degrees each day?

7. Now imagine that the temperature in our classroom is 72 degrees Fahrenheit and the temperature drops 13 degrees each day. Estimate how many days you think it will take for the temperature to reach −129 degrees Fahrenheit.

8. If the temperature is 72 degrees Fahrenheit and drops 13 degrees each day, on which day will the temperature drop to or below the freezing point (32 degrees Fahrenheit)?

9. On which day will the temperature fall below 0 degrees Fahrenheit—a negative temperature?

10. Use the constant counting function feature on your calculator to repeatedly subtract 13 degrees from 72 degrees until you reach a temperature of –129 degrees Fahrenheit. Record how many days it will take to reach the coldest temperature ever recorded.

11. Look back at **The Problem** listed on the first page of the lesson. On a separate sheet of paper, write a letter to a friend who is taking a trip to Antarctica. Tell your friend how much colder it is in Antarctica than in our classroom. Include what you have learned about the freezing point, negative numbers, and the world's coldest recorded temperature.

From the French Bakery
Teacher's Guide

Measurement Concepts: Fractions, conversion between systems

Calculator Focus: Estimating with decimals

Materials:
- From the French Bakery worksheet (one per group; pp. 41–43)
- calculators

Procedure: Students will work in partners or small groups of three to complete the From the French Bakery worksheet. Teachers can use the facilitation questions below to help guide the students as they complete the worksheet.

Vocabulary:
- *metric system of measurement*: a base-10 system of measurement. It was developed in France in the late 1700s and is the major system of measurement in almost every country. One exception is the United States, where the customary system of measurement is used in most everyday situations.
- *customary system of measurement*: the measurement system most commonly used in everyday life in the United States. Colonists from England brought it to this land, although many cultures, some of them dating back to ancient times, contributed to its development.
- *milliliter (mL)*: a unit of capacity in the metric system of measurement; 1,000 milliliters = 1 liter.
- *gram*: a unit of weight in the metric system of measurement.
- *ounce*: a unit of weight or capacity in the customary system of measurement.
- *cup*: a unit of capacity in the customary system of measurement.
- *measurement conversion*: the process of converting from one unit to another.

For instance, 1 milliliter = 0.0338 fluid ounces.

Facilitation Questions:
- *What resources could you use to find out the number of ounces in a gram and fluid ounces in a milliliter?*
- *What are some resources you could use to convert a recipe in another language if it wasn't already converted?*
- *Look at the recipe to see how much flour is required. If there are 0.0353 ounces per gram, how many ounces are there in 110 grams?*
- *How do we need to adjust the recipe so that it makes three times as much batter?*
- *How does knowing how many ounces are in one cup help you figure how many ounces are in $1\frac{1}{2}$ cups?*
- *How will you know how large of a package of flour to buy?*

Answer Key:

2. The customary units for the crêpes recipe should read:
- 3.88 ounces flour (about 4 ounces or ½ cup)
- 6.76 fluid ounces milk (about 7 fluid ounces or ⅞ cup)
- 2.54 fluid ounces water (about 3 fluid ounces or ⅜ cup)
- 2 eggs
- 1.77 ounces butter (about 2 ounces, ¼ cup, or 4 tablespoons)

3. Triple the recipe.

4. The final recipe for 45 crepes should read:
- 1 ½ c. flour
- 2 ⅝ c. milk
- 1 ⅛ c. water
- 6 eggs
- ¾ c. butter

5. Answers will vary. The shopping list may be scored holistically using the Generalized Scoring Rubric.

Name:_____ Date:_____

From the French Bakery

Our class is hosting a group of students from France. We want to make some French food to serve our visitors. We only have a cookbook written in French. Our teacher can translate the French terms but wants us to convert from metric (which they use in France) to customary units of measure (which we use in the United States). How can we create delicious crêpes following the French recipe?

The Problem: How could we figure out how much of each ingredient to use in our crêpes?

Crêpes are a sort of French pancake. They are served with honey, fresh fruit, and whipped topping, or just a squeeze of lemon juice. They taste delicious no matter how you serve them! The recipe for crêpes is first listed in French. Because the French use metric units of measure, we must convert to customary units before we begin cooking.

Name:_____   Date:_____

1. Use the conversion chart to help you fill in the blanks on the English recipe with the correct amounts for each ingredient. The calculator will help you be exact (round to two decimal places).

Conversion Chart

Metric Unit	Customary Unit
0.0353 ounces	1 gram
0.0338 fluid ounces	1 milliliter
8 fluid ounces	1 cup
8 ounces	1 cup

Crêpes

110 grams farine

200 milliliters lait

75 milliliters l'eau

2 oeufs

50 grams beurre

Fais tourner le mixeur 10 secondes. Graisse la poêle avec du beurre et mets-y 2 cuillers à soupe de pâte à crêpe. Fais cuire à feu moyen environ 1 minute. Mets la crêpe dans un plat, courvre-le d'un torchonet pose-le dans un endroit chaud. Pour 15 crêpes environ.

Crêpes

_____ ounces flour

_____ fluid ounces milk

_____ fluid ounces water

_____ eggs

_____ ounces butter

Mix the ingredients for 10 seconds. Heat the pan over medium heat. Grease the pan with some butter and drop 2 tablespoons of batter into the pan. Cook over medium heat about 1 minute. Put it on a plate and keep it warm until ready to serve. Makes about 15 small crêpes.

---

2. Now that we have the recipe converted to customary units, we need to adjust it so that we have enough crêpes for 45 people to eat one crêpe each. How can we adjust the recipe so that it will make enough batter for 45 crêpes?

3. When cooking, many people prefer to use cups rather than fluid ounces or ounces. Also, many cooks round ingredients to the nearest "friendly fraction." For instance, 11.64 fluid ounces could round to 1½ cup rather than 1.45 cups. It just makes things easier in the kitchen. Use your calculator to help you (a) change ounces to cups, rounding to the nearest friendly fraction, such as eighths, fourths, thirds, or halves and (b) adjust the recipe for 45 crepes.

Crêpes for 45 people:

_____ cups flour

_____ cups milk

_____ cups water

_____ eggs

_____ cups butter

4. On a separate sheet, make a shopping list for the ingredients we will need to buy to make our crêpes. Include an amount for each ingredient and don't forget the strawberries or other yummy toppings for the crêpes. C'est délicieux!

Where the Sidewalk Grows
Teacher's Guide

Measurement Concepts: Length, area, perimeter

Calculator Focus: Examining relationships between sets of numbers

Materials:
- Where the Sidewalk Grows worksheet (one per group; pp. 45–46)
- calculators

Procedure: Students will work in partners or small groups of three to complete the Where the Sidewalk Grows worksheet. Teachers can use the facilitation questions below to help guide the students as they complete the worksheet.

Vocabulary:
- *height (length):* usually refers to the measure of the distance vertically from one end of an object to the other.
- *base (width):* usually refers to the measure of the distance horizontally from one end of an object to the other.
- *area:* the amount of space enclosed by a figure; usually expressed in square units.
- *square unit:* a square with each side equal to one unit.
- *perimeter:* the distance around a shape or figure.
- *dimension:* length and width (or height and base) of a shape or figure.

Facilitation Questions:
- *What other experience have you had finding perimeter?*
- *What other experience have you had finding area?*
- *What does the term* area *mean?*
- *How can you find the area of the sidewalk?*
- *What does the term* height *mean?*
- *What does the term* base *mean?*
- *Does the perimeter always change if the area changes?*
- *What are some possible number combinations that would give the sidewalk 320 square feet of area?*

- *How could your calculator help you find number combinations quickly?*
- *What are some patterns you see on the perimeter and area columns of the table in Question 4?*
- *What kind of information do you think the principal would need to know about the new sidewalk?*

Answer Key:

1. The picture should be labeled accurately with a length of 30 feet and a width of 8 feet. The perimeter of the sidewalk is 76 feet.

2. The area of the sidewalk is 240 square feet.

3. The area and perimeter may change if the length and width of the sidewalk change, or the perimeter or area may remain the same. It depends on the dimensions of the sidewalk.

4. The table below contains some possible dimensions for the sidewalk.

Proposed Sidewalk	Height (length)	Base (width)	Perimeter	Area
A	20 feet	16 feet	72 feet	320 square feet
B	32 feet	10 feet	84 feet	320 square feet
C	40 feet	8 feet	96 feet	320 square feet
D	64 feet	5 feet	138 feet	320 square feet
E	80 feet	4 feet	168 feet	320 square feet
F	160 feet	2 feet	324 feet	320 square feet

5. Possible answers include the following: For the same area, the perimeter can vary a lot. The area column usually contains the largest numbers on the table. Area is usually larger than the perimeter but not always.

6. Answers will vary. Score the letter to the principal using the Generalized Scoring Rubric.

Name:_____ Date:_____

Where the Sidewalk Grows

Every afternoon the sidewalk in front of the school is crowded with kids, bikes, teachers, and parents. The principal is thinking about changing the size of the sidewalk in front of the school. How will changing the width and length of the sidewalk affect its area and perimeter?

The Problem: How could we figure out how to increase the space on the sidewalk in front of our school?

---

1. Look at the picture of a sidewalk below. Its dimensions measure 30 feet by 8 feet. Label the dimensions on the picture of the sidewalk. The perimeter of the sidewalk is the distance around the edge. What is the perimeter of the sidewalk?

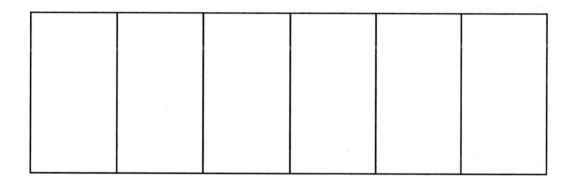

2. The area of the sidewalk is the number of square feet the sidewalk covers. What is the area of the sidewalk shown above?

3. If the principal wants to adjust the size of the sidewalk so that more people can fit on it, how will that affect the perimeter and area?

4. Increasing the area would allow for more people to stand on the sidewalk at the same time. The principal wants to increase the area of the sidewalk to 320 square feet. Use your calculator to find possible lengths and widths for the new sidewalk. Fill in the table with the dimensions.

Proposed Sidewalk	Height (length)	Base (width)	Perimeter	Area
A				320 square feet
B				320 square feet
C				320 square feet
D				320 square feet
E				320 square feet
F				320 square feet

5. Look carefully at the rows and columns of the table. Describe three patterns or relationships you notice between the dimensions of the sidewalk and the perimeter and area of the sidewalk.

6. Which dimensions do you think would be best for the sidewalk? On a separate sheet of paper, write a letter to the principal sharing your ideas for the new sidewalk and how you know the area of the sidewalk will accommodate more people than the old sidewalk did.

Outside the Box
Teacher's Guide

Measurement Concepts: Surface area and volume of rectangular solids

Calculator Focus: Detecting patterns in formulas

Materials:
- Outside the Box worksheet (one per group; pp. 49–53)
- calculators

Procedure: Students will work in partners or small groups of three to complete the Outside the Box worksheet. Teachers can use the facilitation questions below to help guide the students as they complete the worksheet.

Vocabulary:
- *surface area:* the total area of the surface of a space figure. The surface area of a rectangular prism is found by adding the areas of all of the faces.
- *square unit:* a square with each side equal to one unit.
- *volume:* the volume of a space figure is how much space it occupies. The volume of a container is how much it can hold. Volume is often measured in cubic units.
- *cubic units:* each edge of each square face of a cubic unit measures one unit.
- *length:* usually refers to the measure of the distance vertically from one end of an object to the other.
- *width:* usually refers to the measure of the distance horizontally from one end of an object to the other.
- *height:* the altitude of an object; how tall something is.
- *dimension:* length and width (or height and base) of a shape or figure.

Facilitation Questions:
- *Which edge of the box will you label 5 units?*
- *Which edge of the box will you label 3 units?*
- *Which edge of the box will you label 2 units?*

- *What steps could you take to find the surface area of the box?*
- *How many faces does the box have?*
- *What is the area of each face?*
- *When we see an "x" used in a description of size, we usually say the word "by" instead of multiplied by or times. How would you read the dimensions of the dump truck?*
- *What are some patterns you see in the volume answers given in the table?*
- *How could you use your calculator to help you to quickly figure the volume of each box?*
- *A box must be large enough in length, width, and height, as well as volume, in order to fit the gift inside. Also, remember that we are trying to conserve wrapping paper, so choose the smallest box that the gift will fit into. Would Box B be large enough for the pair of shoes?*
- *How could drawing a picture of the box help you figure the surface area?*
- *How could you describe the steps and reasoning used to figure out how much wrapping paper would be needed to cover the box? What kind of details should you include in your letter?*

Answer Key:

1.

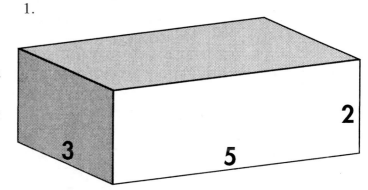

2. 62 square units.
3. Answers will vary. A reasonable estimate will be between 25 and 40 cubes.
4. Answers will vary.

47

5.

Gift	Approximate Size of Gift (Length x Width x Height)	Volume of Gift
Dump truck	4 units x 3 units x 2 units	24 cubic units
Pair of shoes	7 units x 4 units x 3 units	84 cubic units
Box of crayons	3 units x 2 units x 1 unit	6 cubic units
Purse	7 units x 5 units x 2 units	70 cubic units
Doll	9 units x 3 units x 3 units	81 cubic units
Shirt and pants	8 units x 10 units x 5 units	400 cubic units
Socks and underwear	8 units x 7 units x 3 units	168 cubic units
Calculator	2 units x 4 units x 1 unit	8 cubic units
CD player	4 units x 4 units x 1 unit	16 cubic units
Football	5 units x 8 units x 5 units	200 cubic units
Giant Frisbee	20 units x 20 units x 2 units	800 cubic units
Stuffed animal	5 units x 8 units x 4 units	160 cubic units
Jewelry box and necklaces	5 units x 4 units x 6 units	120 cubic units

6.

Box	Dimensions (in Units)	Volume (in Cubic Units)
A	4 x 4 x 4	64
B	6 x 6 x 5	180
C	8 x 8 x 10	640
D	10 x 10 x 10	1,000
E	20 x 20 x 5	2,000

7.

Gift	Matching Box (A, B, etc.)
Dump truck	A
Pair of shoes	C
Box of crayons	A
Purse	C
Doll	D
Shirt and pants	D
Socks and underwear	C
Calculator	A
CD player	A
Football	C
Giant Frisbee	E
Stuffed animal	C
Jewelry box and necklaces	C

8.

Box	Dimensions (in Units)	Surface Area (in Square Units)
A	4 x 4 x 4	96
B	6 x 6 x 5	192
C	8 x 8 x 10	448
D	10 x 10 x 10	600
E	20 x 20 x 5	1,200

9.

Box	Surface Area of Box (in Square Units)	Number of Boxes Needed	Paper Needed to Cover Boxes (in Square Units)
A	96	4	384
B	192	0	0
C	448	6	2,688
D	600	2	1,200
E	1,200	1	1,200

10. We will need 5,472 square units of wrapping paper.

11. Answers will vary. The entire assignment may be scored holistically using the Generalized Scoring Rubric.

Name:_____ Date:_____

Outside the Box

    For the winter holidays, our class is providing gifts for children at the local homeless shelter. We have collected new toys, clothes, shoes, and school supplies. Now we are ready to wrap the gifts. How much paper will we need to wrap our gift boxes?

The Problem: How could we figure out how much paper it will take to wrap our gift boxes for the children's shelter?

1. Look at the picture of the rectangular prism below. The length of the box is 5 units. The width of the box is 3 units. The height of the box is 2 units. Label the box with its dimensions.

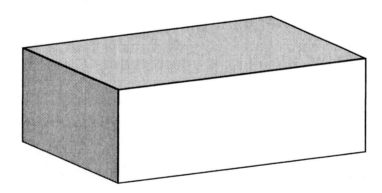

2. The surface area of the box is found by adding the areas of all of the faces. What is the surface area of the box?

Name:_____ Date:_____

3. We can also figure the volume of the box. The volume of a box is how much it can hold. How many unit cubes do you think would fit into the box above?

4. Explain how you decided on your estimate for the number of unit cubes you think would fit into the box above.

5. The table below shows each gift and its approximate dimensions. The volume of some of the gifts is filled in. Look for a pattern. Then use your calculator to fill in the rest of the table.

Gift	Approximate Size of Gift (Length x Width x Height)	Volume of Gift
Dump truck	4 units x 3 units x 2 units	
Pair of shoes	7 units x 4 units x 3 units	
Box of crayons	3 units x 2 units x 1 unit	6 cubic units
Purse	7 units x 5 units x 2 units	
Doll	9 units x 3 units x 3 units	
Shirt and pants	8 units x 10 units x 5 units	400 cubic units
Socks and underwear	8 units x 7 units x 3 units	
Calculator	2 units x 4 units x 1 unit	
CD player	4 units x 4 units x 1 unit	
Football	5 units x 8 units x 5 units	200 cubic units
Giant Frisbee	20 units x 20 units x 2 units	
Stuffed animal	5 units x 8 units x 4 units	
Jewelry box and necklaces	5 units x 4 units x 6 units	120 cubic units

6. A local box company has donated boxes of different sizes for the gifts. Fill in the volume for the boxes in the table below.

Box	Dimensions (in Units)	Volume (in Cubic Units)
A	4 x 4 x 4	
B	6 x 6 x 5	
C	8 x 8 x 10	
D	10 x 10 x 10	
E	20 x 20 x 5	

7. Use the information from the tables in Questions 5 and 6 to help you match a gift to a box. A box must be large enough in length, width, and height, as well as volume in order to fit the gift inside. Also, remember that we are trying to conserve wrapping paper, so choose the smallest box that the gift will fit into.

Gift	Matching Box (A, B, etc.)
Dump truck	
Pair of shoes	
Box of crayons	
Purse	
Doll	
Shirt and pants	
Socks and underwear	
Calculator	
CD player	
Football	
Giant Frisbee	
Stuffed animal	
Jewelry box and necklaces	

Name:_____ Date:_____

8. Now that we have the gifts matched to their boxes, we need to figure out how much wrapping paper we will need. Remember that to find the surface area, we add the areas of all of the faces of a box. Fill in the surface area for each of the boxes in the table below. It may help to draw a picture of the box and label its dimensions.

Box	Dimensions (in Units)	Surface Area (in Square Units)
A	4 x 4 x 4	
B	6 x 6 x 5	
C	8 x 8 x 10	
D	10 x 10 x 10	
E	20 x 20 x 5	

9. Fill in the table to help you organize the information we have about which boxes we will need and the surface area of the boxes. For instance, multiply the surface area of Box A by the number of A boxes needed. This determines the paper needed to cover the A boxes.

Box	Surface Area of Box (in Square Units)	Number of Boxes Needed	Paper Needed to Cover Boxes (in Square Units)
A			
B			
C			
D			
E			

10. Use your calculator to add up the Paper Needed to Cover Boxes column. This will give us the total amount of wrapping paper we need to wrap our gift boxes. Write the total here.

11. Write a letter to a child who will receive one of the gifts. Share with the child how you selected the appropriate box for the gift and how you figured out how much wrapping paper the gift would need.

Jumping for a World Record
Teacher's Guide

Measurement Concept: Time

Calculator Focus: Visualizing large numbers

Materials:

- Jumping for a World Record worksheet (one per group; pp. 55–58)
- clock with second hand or stopwatches
- calculators

Procedure: Students will work in partners or small groups of three to complete the Jumping for a World Record worksheet. Teachers can use the facilitation questions below to help guide the students as they complete the worksheet.

Vocabulary:

- *minute:* a unit of measurement for measuring time; one minute equals 60 seconds.

Facilitation Questions:

- *What do you think would be a reasonable estimate for the number of jumping jacks you could do in one minute?*
- *What is a good benchmark for one minute?*
- *How many times do you estimate you would be able to reach down and touch your toes? Write you name?*
- *What are some factors that might affect the number of jumping jacks a person could do?*
- *Where could we find out how many students there are in each grade at our school?*
- *How could you use your calculator to help you figure how many jumping jacks the entire grade of kindergarten could do?*
- *How could you use your calculator to help you figure how many jumping jacks the whole school could do in one minute?*

- *How does the number of jumping jacks a sixth grader can do compare to the number of jumping jacks a second grader can do?*
- *According to your table, which class contributes most to the grand total?*
- *How could you use your calculator to help you figure how close we are to the world record for jumping jacks?*
- *If we doubled our total each day, how many jumping jacks could we do on the third day?*

Answer Key:

1. Answers will vary but should be reasonable, falling between 15 and 60.
2. Answers will vary but may include television commercials that last one minute or other activities that require one minute, such as walking from the front door of the school to the main office.
3. Answers will vary.
4. Students should calculate the numerical difference between their estimate and their actual number of jumping jacks and make a comment about the magnitude of the difference (e.g., I thought I could do 100 jumping jacks, but I was only able to do 40.).
5. Some children may not have had experience doing jumping jacks. This would probably affect the number of jumping jacks they could do in one minute.
6–10. Answers will vary.
11. On the third day, the kindergartner could do more jumping jacks than a sixth grader.
12. 7,680 jumping jacks.
13. Answers will vary but the response should be double the number of jumping jacks the entire school could do (the bottom right box on the table in Question 9).
14–15. Answers will vary.

Name:_____ Date:_____

Jumping for a World Record

Our school wants to break the world record for the most jumping jacks completed in a minute. The current record is 59,463. We need to figure out if it is possible for our school to become the new record holder.

The Problem: How could we figure out how many jumping jacks everyone in our school could do in one minute?

1. How many jumping jacks do you think you can you do in one minute? Write your estimate here.

2. Do you have any benchmarks for the length of one minute? Write about them here.

3. Work with a partner. Have your partner time you as you do jumping jacks for one minute. Count your jumping jacks. Record your number.

4. How does your estimate from Question 1 compare to the actual number of jumping jacks you were able to do?

5. Do you think all kids can do exactly the same number of jumping jacks in one minute as you did? Why or why not?

6. Complete the table below by filling in the number of children in each grade in our school. Some schools do not include all of the grades listed. If your school does not include a grade listed, leave it blank.

Grade	Average Number of Jumping Jacks in One Minute	Number of Kids per Grade	Total Jumping Jacks per Grade
Kindergarten	15		
First Grade	18		
Second Grade	22		
Third Grade	27		
Fourth Grade	33		
Fifth Grade	40		
Sixth Grade	48		
Total Jumping Jacks Whole School			

7. Use your calculator and the information in the table to find the number of jumping jacks the kids in each grade would be able to do in one minute.

8. What number patterns do you see in the table?

Name:_____ Date:_____

9. Add the total jumping jacks for each grade to find the total number of jumping jacks our school could do in one minute. Write this number here and in the bottom righthand box on the table.

10. Based on what you have calculated, will our school be able to break the world record for the most jumping jacks done in one minute? How close will we be to the record?

11. What if the number of jumping jacks a kindergartner did in one minute followed a simple pattern. Imagine that the first day, the kindergartner did 15 jumping jacks in one minute. On the second day, the kindergartner did double the number of jumping jacks from the previous day. If the kindergartner were able to follow this pattern of jumping jacks, how many days would it take for him to do more than a sixth grader could do?

Name:_____ Date:_____

12. Use your calculator to help you figure out how many jumping jacks a kindergartner could do on the 10th day.

13. Now imagine that the entire school followed this doubling pattern. How many jumping jacks could our entire school do on the second day?

14. If the doubling pattern continued, how many days would it take our school to reach the world record?

15. Use your calculator to help you figure out how many jumping jacks the entire school could do on the 10th day.

Name:_____ Date:_____

Appendix A
Generalized Scoring Rubric

	Distinguished	Proficient	Novice	Emergent
Completion	Fully and accurately completes all elements of task.	Fully completes all elements of task with few errors.	Partially completes task with several errors.	Many elements of the task are incomplete or incorrect.
Mathematical Communication	Mathematical communication is clear.	Mathematical communication is adequate but somewhat unclear.	Mathematical communication is unclear.	Mathematical communication is very unclear or is not present.

Appendix B
Links to Literature Guide

General Measurement

Millions to Measure by David M. Schwartz, 2006, ISBN# 0-06084-806-5

Ask students what other needs for measurement there are besides length, distance, weight, and volume. Have students invent or imagine their own magicians to introduce a friend to temperature, money, and other forms of measurement.

Time

Clocks and More Clocks by Pat Hutchins, 1994, ISBN# 0-02745-921-7

Have students investigate how long it takes to do everyday activities. For instance, ask them to first estimate and then time how long it takes for them to get from their bedroom to the kitchen or from home to school. Have the students chart the results and write about their experience.

Let It Shine: Stories of Black Women Freedom Fighters by Andrea Davis Pinkney, 2001, ISBN# 0-43933-220-6

Have students create a timeline for the stories of the Black women freedom fighters, then have students create their own personal timelines highlighting important events in their own lives.

Somewhere in the World Right Now by Stacey Schuett, 1997, ISBN# 0-67988-549-8

Have students refer to a map of the United States to draw in the appropriate time zones. Then have students expand the map to include the entire world's time zones and the International Date Line.

Size of an Angle

Sir Cumference and the Great Knight of Angleland: A Math Adventure by Cindy Neuschwander, 2001, ISBN# 1-57091-169-X

Have students invent their own hero to investigate the angles they see in the classroom. Then have students write a story and illustrate it with pictures of the angles they find.

Sir Cumference and the Dragon of Pi: A Math Adventure by Cindy Neuschwander, 1999, ISBN# 1-57091-164-9

Have a Pi Day Celebration on March 14. As a class, bake pies of varying sizes. Assign groups of students to record the diameter, radius, and circumference of one pie on a chart or table. Compile the measurement data from all of the pies into one whole class table and look for patterns. Allow students to use this experience to discover pi.

Temperature

Chinook! by Michael O. Tunnell, 1993, ISBN# 0-68810-869-5

Using the Internet or a weather almanac as a resource, have students research weather patterns before and after a chinook. Students should write about how much the temperature varies before, during, and after a chinook and make comparisons.

Arctic Lights, Arctic Nights by Debbie S. Miller, 2007, ISBN# 0-80279-636-2

Have students examine how the amount of daylight affects the temperature in the Arctic. Students can use the Internet or a weather almanac to make a chart showing the average hours of daylight per month and the average temperature. Students should then make conjectures about how daylight and temperature are related.

Length/Distance

How Tall? by Nicholas Harris, 2004, ISBN# 1-41030-194-X

Provide students with record books or encyclopedias to find amazing measures for weight, temperature, volume, and other types of measurements. As a class, create a picture book to share with younger students who are just beginning to learn about measurement and comparisons.

How Big Is a Foot? by Rolf Myller, 1991, ISBN# 0-44040-495-9

As a class, compare the lengths of several students' feet. Discuss the importance of standardization of units. Have students write a funny story using a unit other than feet (degrees, cents, minutes) to show what might happen if units were not standardized.

My Place in Space by Robin Hirst and Sally Hirst, 1992, ISBN# 0-53107-030-1

Ask students to make a picture book showing their responses to the following questions: If you were traveling at 50 miles per hour, how long would it take to get from where you are to Mount Rushmore? To the center of the Northern Hemisphere? To the center of the Earth? To the center of the solar system? To the center of the galaxy?

Well, a Crocodile Can! by Malachy Doyle, 2000, ISBN# 0-76131-032-0

From reading the book, students will learn that a flea can jump 90 times its height and that a chameleon's tongue is as long as its body. Work in small groups using the Internet or a children's encyclopedia of animal facts to create a collage of other amazing animal measurements.

Daphne Eloise Slater, Who's Tall for Her Age by Gina Willner-Pardo, 1997, ISBN# 0-39573-080-5

As a class, discuss patterns of growth and the influence of genetics, nutrition, and other factors on growth. Use the Internet or other resource to gather data regarding height and weight according to country. Have students make conjectures as to why people living in some countries may be taller or heavier than people living in other countries.

Two Old Potatoes and Me by John Coy, 2003, ISBN# 0-37582-180-5

Provide groups of students with materials to plant and care for a potato plant. Have groups create a table and graph to show the growth of their potato plant over time. At harvest time, prepare a potato feast.

Measuring Penny by Loreen Leedy, 2000, ISBN# 0-80506-572-5

Have students measure their own pets at home using standard and nonstandard units and create a chart or table with results to share with the class.

Sir Cumference and the First Round Table: A Math Adventure by Cindy Neuschwander, 1997, ISBN# 1-57091-152-5

Have small groups of students use a piece of yarn or string to measure the diameter, radius, and circumference of four circular faces. Make a chart recording the measurements gathered by the whole class. Have students look for and write about patterns they see in the three measurements.

Money

Pigs Will Be Pigs: Fun With Math and Money by Amy Axelrod, 1997, ISBN# 0-68981-219-1

Have students write about how they would spend their money if they were one of the pigs in the story. Have students make up their own restaurant, creating a unique menu and prices. Then have students trade menus with a partner to spend their money.

How the Second Grade Got $8,205.50 to Visit the Statue of Liberty by Nathan Zimelman, 1992, ISBN# 0-80753-431-5

Discuss with the class how long they think it would take to save enough money to visit the Statue of Liberty. Have students write up a proposal to give to the principal. The proposal might include what types of projects their class could do to earn money for the trip and how much money they could earn from each project.

The Go-Around Dollar by Barbara Johnston Adams, 1992, ISBN# 0-02700-031-1

Work as a class to trace the journey of the dollar on a map. Have students design their own dollar bill and write a short story of their bill's amazing journey.

Alexander, Who Used to be Rich Last Sunday by Judith Viorst, 1987, ISBN# 0-68971-199-9

As the story is read aloud, have students use real or manipulative coins to follow the action of the story. Have students create a chart to record the values of the coins and how much money Alexander has left.

If You Made a Million by David M. Schwartz, 1994, ISBN# 0-68813-634-6

Have students write a five-line poem about how they would spend $1 million. Use the Internet to investigate the antifraud safeguards on new American currency. Show students how to compare interest rates in a newspaper's real estate section.

The Penny Pot by Stuart J. Murphy, 1998, ISBN# 0-06446-717-1

Ask students what games and booths they would like to visit at the school fair. Have them design a poster advertising the booths and the price for each activity. Write a paragraph describing how they set the price for each booth.

Weight

Who Sank the Boat? by Pamela Allen, 1996, ISBN# 0-69811-373-X

Provide students with materials to explore concepts of volume, circumference, and area using boxes (pizza, cereal, or shoes), scoops, lids, spoons, birdseed, rice, beans, sand, and water. Have students write about their experiences in a booklet they can share with their parents.

Actual Size by Steve Jenkins, 2004, ISBN# 0-61837-594-5

Have students make a chart comparing the sizes of animals from birth to adulthood, comparing different species. As a class, discuss how size can be an adaptation that helps the animal survive.

What Would Mama Do? by Judith Ross Enderle and Stephanie G. Tessler, 1995, ISBN# 1-56397-418-5

Provide students with materials such as water, rice, and beans to investigate equivalencies in the customary system for liquids, dry materials, and measures of weight. Have students write about their investigation of equivalence in a booklet they can share with their parents.

About the Author

Carrie S. Cutler, Ed.D., is passionate about mathematics education and the calculator's unique potential to bring the real world into the math classroom. In her work as a professor and consultant, Cutler strives to make math engaging and understandable for children and adults. She holds degrees from Utah State University, Brigham Young University, and University of Houston. Cutler currently lives in The Woodlands, TX, with her husband and five children.